Vision Works is a masterful collection of real-life stories and practical tools that help business owners gain traction in their business.

—Gino Wickman
Author of *Traction* and *Entrepreneurial Leap*

Vision Works is a crystal clear and profoundly useful book...a super-practical system for dropping the victim mentality and achieving real, bottom-line results.

—Steve Chandler
Best-Selling Author, Motivational Speaker

Alex Freytag and the ProfitWorks team work side by side with executives and business owners facing the challenges of turning vision into managed enterprises. *Vision Works* is the place to start for guidance on what to study, whom to follow, and how to proceed.

—Artie Isaac
Executive Coach, Speaker, Trainer

Vision Works offers a clear, concise message that works in the real world. Alex's guidance is working for our management team, our associates, and our stakeholders.

—Ted Coons
Chairman and CEO, Spillman Company

Alex offers impactful leadership tools and practices that any results-driven leader can immediately put into action.

—Nataline Lomedico
CEO and President, Giroux Glass, Inc.

Vision Works is a comprehensive summary and resource that sets the stage for entrepreneurs to share their vision and lead their teams to success!

—Sandy L. King
President, Symbiont Service Corporation

VISION WORKS

Awaken the Earning Mindset, Bridge the Missing Profit Link, and Cultivate Untapped Potential

ALSO BY ALEX FREYTAG

Profit Works: Unravel the Complexity of Incentive Plans to Increase Employee Productivity, Cultivate an Engaged Workforce, and Maximize Your Company's Potential

co-authored with Tom Bouwer

See the end of this book for a sample chapter.

Look for more books from Alex Freytag in the near future.

VISION WORKS

Awaken the Earning Mindset, Bridge the Missing Profit Link, and Cultivate Untapped Potential

Alex Freytag

ethos
collective

Published by Ethos Collective
PO Box 43, Powell, OH 43065
www.EthosCollective.vip

LCCN: 2020925123

ISBN: 978-1-63680-018-9 (paperback)
ISBN: 978-1-63680-019-6 (hardback)
ISBN: 978-1-63680-020-2 (ebook)

Available in paperback, hardback, e-book, and audiobook

Any Internet addresses (websites, blogs, etc.) and telephone numbers printed in this book are offered as a resource. They are not intended in any way to be or imply an endorsement by Ethos Collective, nor does Ethos Collective vouch for the content of these sites and numbers for the life of this book.

Some names and identifying details have been changed to protect the privacy of individuals.

This book is dedicated to the late
Donald A. Freytag.

You remain an inspiration, Dad.

CONTENTS

INTRODUCTION

My business partner, Tom, and I were four days into our third annual Clarity Trip™ in Peru and we were exhausted. We were hiking eighty-six miles toward Machu Picchu with a Peruvian guide named Oliver, and we were out of water. Oliver promised us that our campsite was just around the corner, but after two hours and six unexpected switchbacks, our water bottles weren't the only things that were empty; our energy and our faith in Oliver were drained. His credibility as our leader and our trust in him stood at a negative balance.

These Clarity Trips were an annual tradition we'd sort of fallen into a few years earlier. In 2014, Tom was planning to hike to the top of Mount Kilimanjaro, and I asked if I could join him. I had no idea what I was signing up for. He agreed to let me come along and we had a game-changing experience getting to the top together. If you have ever considered the ultimate team health activity, climbing Kili is it.

In 2015, we hiked seventy-six miles on the incessantly rainy Appalachian Trail and then undertook our rather unbalanced trip to Peru the next year. We will share all the gory details about Clarity Trips in a future book, but we absolutely believe that these trips have made us better business partners and better versions of ourselves.

Tom and I spent nine years as business partners. We worked with hundreds of entrepreneurial companies to help leadership teams implement and run their businesses on the Entrepreneurial Operating System® (EOS®) and create cultures where employees think and act like owners. As an Expert EOS Implementer®, I coach leadership teams to get alignment on their vision, to create accountability and discipline that help them achieve their vision, and to do so as a healthy, functional, cohesive team.

> **A consistent theme has emerged around the incredible challenge that business owners have in engaging their employees in a shared vision.**

During the countless conversations we've had on the trail about our various client experiences over the last twenty-five years, a consistent theme has emerged around the incredible challenge that business owners have in engaging their employees in a shared vision. This challenge leads to many related questions:

1. Why do so many employees have an entitlement mentality? **How do you "awaken" your employees toward an earning mindset?**

2. Why is there such a weak link between employees' leading, daily activities and the company's lagging financial results? **How do you "bridge" this missing "profit link"?**

3. Why don't more business owners unlock the potential of their workforce? **How do you**

"cultivate" the untapped potential that exists in the minds of your workforce?

I wrote this book to share ideas, discuss these common challenges, and help business owners like you address them. I mention several other authors whose work has contributed greatly to the ideas I discuss in this book. I encourage you to read their work as well for a deeper dive.

In addition to sharing some of my experiences, my ultimate goal is to inspire you to implement these methods to gain more control, experience more traction, and achieve your vision.

For over twenty-five years, I have been passionate about being a hero to entrepreneurs. I love everything about entrepreneurship. In high school I designed and sold James Dean T-shirts. After college I painted houses in Los Angeles while pursuing an acting career. I started ProfitWorks in 1996 with my brother, and we went without a paycheck for nearly seven years while pursuing a business in which we saw so much potential. Oddly, I never considered myself an entrepreneur until I left a bureaucratic

$500 million organization to serve at the right hand of a visionary entrepreneur who was running a small business that taught employees to think and act like owners.

I believe entrepreneurs are the lifeblood of a market economy. Like the mythical Atlas, they hold the weight of the world upon their shoulders. You and I both know it's no walk in the park. It's a true responsibility, as there are so many families depending on our commitment to our dreams. And onward we march.

Ultimately, I want to help you build a better business and a better life for yourself. I want you to be in love with your business, and I hope you find this book valuable and inspiring. Let's get started with my discovery!

CHAPTER 1

THE LEADERSHIP TEAM IS BROKEN

In early 1995, my father shared a business idea he had with my older brother and me. He'd been in business for many years and felt that most employees had no idea a) how a company makes money or b) how much (or how little) profit companies truly make. As a board member with the Central Ohio Center for Economic Education, he periodically interacted with university economics professors whose mission was to teach primary school teachers how to teach economics to kids.

A consummate entrepreneur, he thought that perhaps there was a business idea in teaching employees about economics, business, and finance to help them begin to see the business from an owner's perspective. My brother and I thought this was a great idea, so we created a business plan and launched a company called ProfitWorks in 1996.

Although the initial idea centered around training employees on economics and business, we quickly realized that for the lessons to have an impact, we would have to include some real financial data from our clients' companies.

In recent years, the fear of sharing financial information with employees has waned a bit, but initially we found there was a great deal of trepidation. Business owners asked us:

- What if I teach my employees about profit and then they leave?

- What if I don't teach them and they stay?

- What if they share the information with our competitors?

- What's the purpose of sharing the information? They won't understand it anyway.

- Why should I care if my employees understand this stuff?

As you can imagine, many business owners were not excited about the idea of sharing financial information with their employees, but we discovered that truly enlightened business owners could see the value. Over the years, I have learned that the owners of the best companies put their fears aside. These leaders realize that when their employees have good information, they make better decisions. They also realize the correlated positive effect: when they share more information with their employees, they build trust with their workforce, and the barrier between "us" and "them" lowers as open and honest communication increases.

> **Leaders realize that when their employees have good information, they make better decisions.**

The content of our original workshops began with the basic fact that profit is the engine of growth in a market economy. Without profit, there is no incentive for anyone—owners, investors, management, or employees. We developed content around this fundamental truth of profit motivation as a potential reward for risk taken. We included exercises to teach employees about risk, return, and liquidity, and the interrelationship of the three.

In the late 1990s, I met a man named Jack Stack, who had published *The Great Game of Business* in 1994. I attended his annual gathering in Springfield, Missouri, and learned a considerable amount about the path great companies can take to engage their employees in transforming their businesses. I also met and worked with Brad Hams, who founded a company called Ownership Thinking and who published a book by the same name in 2012. These visionaries, and others like them who had similar ideas about teaching employees about business, have the same basic goal as I do: improve the financial performance of a company by helping employees understand and focus on the measurables that they can affect. We all emphasize that financial literacy is *not* just about sharing financial information; it's about truly reaching the employees, inspiring them, and getting their hearts into the business. We know that financial literacy strongly improves culture.

Today we call this type of company "healthy and smart." Most businesses are smart. They know how to deliver their product or service and make money. They are financially focused, and that's great. But most companies are not healthy. "Healthy" is about culture. "Healthy" is about solving business issues without blame or finger-pointing. It is about forming a united front and eliminating politics. It requires team members to be open and honest. Companies of excellence—truly great companies—are both healthy and smart.

Healthy and Smart

After a few years of working with companies to help them implement our business literacy and employee engagement system, I noticed a disturbing trend. I was getting calls from about half of the owners we had trained three to six months later saying, "Alex, your system isn't working!" We had designed scorecards and taught their leadership teams about measurables and the importance of having regular meetings, so I would naturally ask, "Tell me how your weekly meetings are going. Are you using the scorecard and forecasting against your budget?" The panicked owners would inevitably say, "Well, we haven't started having our meetings yet." As our conversation progressed, I would undoubtedly learn that the owners and their teams were not using many, if any, of the employee engagement tools that we had developed together.

My discovery was this: it wasn't that the system wasn't working—the leadership team was broken! I found that leadership team members were often rowing in different directions. They were usually undisciplined and overwhelmed by the day-to-day whirlwind. They didn't hold each other accountable, and in many cases, they didn't believe that the employee engagement tools would work, so they didn't drive them.

Can you imagine asking your employees to follow you when you and your leadership team don't know or agree on where you're going?

CHAPTER 2

CREDIBILITY AND TRUST

In so many cases, members of the leadership team of an organization are not on the same page, or worse, they are so misaligned that their dysfunction completely sabotages any system's potential for success, as well as the company's potential.

When your leadership team is completely aligned on where you are going and how you are going to get there, you have clarity. When your leadership team communicates that clarity to your entire company, you build credibility within the workforce. This idea of credibility is critical to establishing the potential for trust; trust is the core of culture and success. It is the core of any relationship. Without trust, you have no foundation upon which to build a thriving organization.

In *The 7 Habits of Highly Effective People*, Stephen R. Covey talks about a trust account that exists between two individuals. Each individual makes deposits into the metaphorical trust account that helps nurture the relationship, and the relationship naturally grows. In the same way, individuals can make withdrawals from the trust account.

> **This idea of credibility is critical to establishing the potential for trust; trust is the core of culture and success.**

If you imagine a married couple, you can see how this metaphor plays out. The husband cooks dinner; he makes a deposit. The wife buys a pair of shoes for her husband that she thinks he might like; she makes a deposit. The husband forgets to tell his wife about an evening meeting and misses a planned family dinner; he makes a withdrawal. And so on. As long as there is a positive balance in the trust account, the relationship is usually not significantly damaged by these occasional withdrawals.

The same trust account can be said to exist between a leadership team and the workforce. The trust account offers great potential for the company. Any company that is not building this account with the workforce is missing a huge opportunity. The following table identifies some of the Trust Builders and Trust Destroyers I commonly see in the workplace.

Trust Builders	Trust Destroyers
Transparency	Hidden agendas
Follow through	Say one thing and do another
Open and honest	Disrespect —Shooting down people/ideas
A handful of rules	Politics
Delegation	Micro-management
Fairness	Changing the rules in the middle of the game
A results-based workplace	A time-based workplace

Trust Builders and Destroyers

What are the net effects of trust? In my experience, trust frees people. It provides autonomy. Dan Pink, author of *Drive*, says that autonomy is one of the three elements that truly motivates people (the others are mastery and purpose). Trust provides that autonomy. When people truly feel trusted, they begin to take more risks; they learn, grow, feel pride, and experience the joy of accomplishment.

Likewise, when someone feels trusted, they intrinsically experience a sense of wholeness. They feel like they are part of a winning team with a common direction. They feel camaraderie with their team, respect, and a sense of belonging, which are near the top in Abraham Maslow's hierarchy of needs.

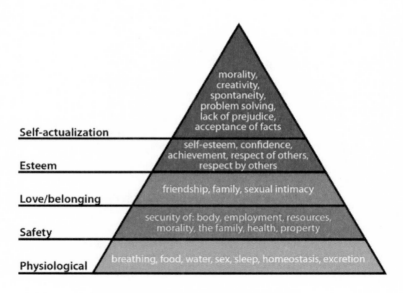

Maslow's Hierarchy of Needs

At the peak of Maslow's pyramid are growth needs, which are reflected in our innate desire to learn and grow once our deficiency needs (physiological, safety, belonging, and esteem) are met. The need for growth and the drive toward self-actualization require special characteristics of an individual if they are to reach their fullest potential.

A lack of trust in the workplace is a leadership issue. Gallup's most recent (2020) annual survey[1] indicated (yet again) that 60 percent of employees are not engaged in their company. In fact, 13 percent are actively disengaged, meaning they may actually work to sabotage the company. Each year, this same research continues to reveal that a top reason that employees quit a company, or worse, "quit and stay" at a company, is a "boss from hell."[2]

A terrible manager doesn't inspire employees, and this leads to unengaged or even actively, deliberately disengaged employees. This in turn can lead to a less safe work environment, waste, quality defects, poor

---

[1]   https://www.gallup.com/workplace/316064/
      employee-engagement-hits-new-high-historic-drop.aspx
[2]   https://bit.ly/3qcmChM

customer service, and even an increase in healthcare costs. All of these erode trust in the workplace, and when there is an absence of trust, it is impossible to build a healthy culture. The Great Place to Work® Institute finds results similar to the Gallup survey, concluding that trust is the core around which the triad of credibility, fairness, and respect are in balance.

Like in any new relationship, trust is one element of a healthy culture that must be nurtured and developed deliberately. Depending on where you are starting, it can take months if not years to develop this level of trust. Keep in mind that you're looking for progress, not perfection.

Culture is defined as the shared values and beliefs of employees that are reflected in their behavior:

- how they go about doing their work

- how they interact with one another

- how they interact with customers

You have a choice with culture: you can let it evolve unintentionally and you'll get what you get, or you can decide to make purposeful choices that will build an intentional culture at your company. Your culture is a choice.

If a culture is left to evolve naturally, or perhaps turned over to HR to decide, the unintended outcome will be a culture that reflects the influence of many individuals rather than one based on intentional values and beliefs shared by a unified tribe. Culture creation is a leadership responsibility, and as Jason Fried and David Heinemeier Hansson say in *Rework*, "Culture is the by-product of consistent behavior." You've got to walk the talk.

Cultural alignment becomes a sustainable competitive advantage that causes a company to surpass others in their industry and build a winning culture.

Here is an example: A few years ago, one of our clients implemented both our employee engagement process (now called The ProfitLink Solution™), as well as EOS. The results were astounding. In the printing industry, where margins are typically 2–3 percent, this company was consistently achieving 8–10 percent margins, and they are having a ton of fun in the process, often winning "Best Place to Work" awards.

Conversely, I worked with a leadership team of a small office furniture distributor. They were searching for a way to help energize the team and really felt that an employee engagement system was the right answer. I customized a program for the company, taught the employees some basic financial concepts, identified measurables, developed scorecards, mini games, and an incentive plan, and set them up with a system for effective meetings.

Unfortunately, after I left, the leadership team didn't use the scorecard. They didn't change their behavior. They didn't execute the mini games. They didn't communicate further with the employees. Employees who were so energized and optimistic during the implementation phase began to lose hope, and they lost faith in the management team. A few of the employees contacted me independently, asking what they should do. The management team had lost credibility and the culture began to crumble. They didn't do what they said they would do.

What I learned was that the company first needed alignment around a vision. The leaders needed to get on the same page, get clarity about where they were going, and then communicate that clarity to the workforce. Only then would the workforce have a better chance of engaging. The owners and leadership team needed to inspire their employees, give everyone direction and focus, and make sure that all of the employees were 100 percent clear on where the company was going and how it was going to get there.

How can you expect someone to follow you if you don't know where you are going? Likewise, if you do know where you are going but don't communicate that to your organization, how can you expect your workforce to feel connected to your vision? It's like asking people to "see what you're saying." Your vision is in your head, but your team can't see what's in your head. It is crucial that you communicate the vision in order to achieve clarity and attain alignment on that vision.

Under the ProfitWorks umbrella, we created a framework that blends leadership team alignment with employee engagement. This new system, The ProfitLink Solution™, creates complete cultural alignment and produces better results.

CHAPTER 3

LEADERSHIP TEAM ALIGNMENT

In *The Truth About Leadership*, James Kouzes and Barry Posner write, "If you think you're a leader and you turn around and no one is following you, then you're simply out for a walk."

In 2011, one of my clients introduced me to a leadership team alignment system called EOS. EOS is a holistic business operating system with real, simple, practical business tools that allow you to simplify, clarify, and align all the pieces of your business to produce your desired results.

EOS helps leadership teams get crystal clear about where the company is going and how they are going to get there. While reading *Traction*, by Gino Wickman, I had a light bulb moment: EOS was the answer for so many business owners who wanted to successfully engage their employees and build a culture of accountability, credibility, trust, and profit.

As Gino Wickman developed the EOS Model®, he realized that any issue an entrepreneur encounters falls into one of Six Key Components™: Vision, People, Data, Issues, Process, and Traction®.

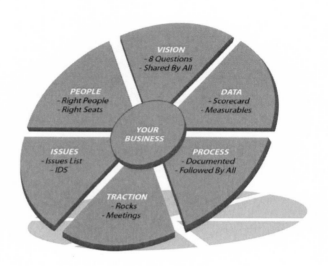

EOS Model

To the degree that you can become strong, 100 percent strong, in each of these components, EOS can help you improve in three ways: Vision, Traction, and Healthy.

- Vision: EOS gets your leadership team 100 percent on the same page with the vision for your organization: who you are, what you do, where you are going, and how you will get there.

- Traction: EOS helps your leadership team become more disciplined and accountable, executing consistently to get more done and achieve every piece of your vision.

- Healthy: EOS helps your leadership team become a healthy, functional, cohesive team, because leaders often don't function well together as a team.

As we like to say, from there, as goes your leadership team so goes the rest of your organization. By effectively implementing this set of tools, the entire organization becomes focused and engaged and shares a common vision. Team members throughout the organization will be disciplined and accountable as they execute well and advance as a healthy team.

Each of the six components of EOS has two key disciplines. Within the first component, Vision, the first key discipline is to answer The 8 Questions™ with your leadership team. The 8 Questions are:

1. What are your Core Values?

2. What is your Core Focus™?

3. What is your 10-Year Target™?

4. What is your Marketing Strategy?

5. What is your 3-Year Picture™?

6. What is your 1-Year Plan?

7. What are your quarterly Rocks?

8. What are your Issues?

When your leadership team becomes crystal clear and 100 percent aligned on the answers to these questions, the culture of your company changes in an incredible way. The tool we use to help the leadership team organize the answers to The 8 Questions is called the Vision/Traction Organizer™ or V/TO™. Once The 8 Questions have been answered, it is important that this vision is shared by everyone in your company, which is the second discipline within the Vision Component™, Shared By All (SBA), which is detailed in the next chapter.

The second component of EOS is People, arguably the root of most issues in any organization. The two disciplines within this component are "Right People" and "Right Seats." As an organization, you must have both. "Right People" means you have people in your organization who understand and act in alignment with the core values that you have identified for your organization. If you have people in your organization who do not share the company's core values, it doesn't mean they are bad people, it just means they aren't a good fit for your culture. Square peg, round hole. When you remove these "misfits" from your culture, it frees you (and them), and you can pursue people who are more in line with your core values and your organization.

> **When you remove these "misfits" from your culture, it frees you (and them), and you can pursue people who are more in line with your core values.**

"Right Seats" means you have developed an Accountability Chart™ that clearly outlines the roles and responsibilities for each seat in your company. The Accountability Chart is an organizational chart on steroids. It's not just about reporting structure. It outlines your team's agreement on what the key roles are for every seat in your organization. I suggest you define the right structure for your organization before you add names. Do not build your Accountability Chart around the people you have. Focus on structure first, people second.

Once these seats have been defined and the names have been added to the chart, you need to determine if the people in your organization are in the right seat as you have defined it in the roles and responsibilities for each seat. This means they "Get the role," they "Want the role," and they have the "Capacity to do the job." Pro tip: they need to have all three.

If you have someone who shares your core values but they can't do the job, you need to make a change. And when you've got someone who can do the job, perhaps very well, but they don't share your core values, again, you have to make a change. The longer you allow either of these issues to fester, the more you act as an anchor for your company, holding it back, reducing your potential for growth, and remaining mired in mediocrity. Within EOS, the People Analyzer™ is a powerful tool you can use to help guide your decisions around this. It allows you to measure your team against your core values and also against the "Right Seats" tool. It is a very powerful, black and white tool that enables healthy coaching conversations with your team members.

The third component of EOS is Data; the two disciplines within this component are the scorecard and the measurables. Whether you call them dashboards, scorecards, key performance indicators (KPI), or measurables is not important. What is important is that your method of choice is clear, simple, and easy to use. I suggest listing five to fifteen measurables on the leadership scorecard and including leading indicators and a few of the typical lagging indicators. Each measurable should be owned by the person who has the greatest influence over the area, whether or not they have the easiest access to it. This way, if there is an issue related to the measurable, this "owner" can do something to solve the issue, or at least move it toward resolution.

When your team is moving toward 100 percent strong in the Vision, People, and Data Components™, your organization, now much more lucid, open, and honest, can more clearly identify barriers and impurities that cause friction or headaches in the daily grind. Within EOS, these are called Issues. Your company's success toward achieving your vision is directly related to your ability to solve Issues.

Issues is the fourth component of EOS. The two key disciplines are simply getting in the habit of establishing and using an Issues List in every meeting and at every level of your organization and using an issue processing track called IDS™. IDS stands for Identify, Discuss, and Solve. Most leadership teams spend their time discussing the heck out of Issues, but rarely do they move to permanent solutions. Great teams acknowledge reality and avoid blame and finger-pointing. They focus on the future, move toward solutions quickly, and knock down a lot of Issues in a short amount of time. Working through Issues in an open and honest way with your team will breathe new life into your meetings and your company.

The fifth component is the Process Component™, which is probably the most overlooked aspect of business. Many leaders feel that going over processes is just delving into minutiae, or they assume that everyone already knows the processes. After you and your team have settled on the names of the handful of core processes that exist in your business, the two key disciplines of Process are documenting those core processes at a high level (entrepreneurial documentation) and then making sure everyone is following them (Followed By All). When I say at a high level, I suggest documenting 20 percent of the steps that will get you 80 percent of the way there, which should result in a few pages of documentation (not hundreds!) per process.

The final component of EOS is Traction. This is where it all comes together and where the magic happens. The two key disciplines are Rocks and Meetings. Rocks are simply the three to seven priorities (less is more) that each member of your leadership team wants to accomplish in the next 90 days. These priorities are critical projects, typically above and beyond the daily whirlwind of the roles and responsibilities of their jobs.

> **If you are truly honest and open in these meetings, the numbers will inevitably move in the right direction.**

The second discipline of the Traction Component is Meetings. The Level 10 Meeting™ is the weekly meeting for your leadership team during which everyone uses all of the tools to hold each other accountable, helps each other stay on track, and identifies and solves any issues that may be holding the company back. The Level 10 Meetings are an incredible discipline. After several weeks of holding these, your leadership team will feel a sense of clarity, openness, and perspective on the business. Ideally, if you are truly honest and open in these meetings, the numbers will inevitably move in the right direction as well.

EOS is unique because it is easy to understand and use, and it holistically addresses all issues rather than applying spot treatments. It works in any entrepreneurial company and across all business models because the system is founded on time-tested methods and principles, not business management theories or flavor-of-the-month fads. It provides a comprehensive way of running your business, and just as important, it provides a foundation of credibility upon which you can build a truly engaged workforce.

CHAPTER 4

EMPLOYEE ENGAGEMENT

Within the EOS Model, we talk about a vision that is *shared by all* (SBA) and processes that are *followed by all* (FBA). These are not trivial matters. Whether you have ten seats on your bus or five hundred seats, it is critical that every one of these people shares your vision, believes your vision, and is rowing in the same direction with you to achieve your vision.

Once you're running on an operating system, the next step toward engaging everyone in the organization toward sharing your vision is to teach them a little bit about business. Business literacy is critical because most employees have never been taught about business and make erroneous assumptions about how much profit a company makes. These assumptions affect their behavior, usually in a very negative way.

> **Most employees have never been taught about business and make erroneous assumptions.**

Since 1996, we have asked employees, "What percent of sales is profit?" Their answers may surprise you; most employees think profit is 30–50 percent of sales! When your employees think your company is making this much profit, they often feel bitter and resentful because they feel they are not making enough money, and someone else is—you! They think you are making all the money off their hard work, and this perpetuates division and mistrust in the culture, not to mention a lack of credibility. Additionally, if they think your company is rolling in the dough, they tend to not be tuned into waste: wasted time, wasted materials, inefficiencies, etc. Finally, this will lead your employees to believe that your company has a money tree or an unlimited source of funds. This belief often reinforces a mentality of entitlement.

Of course, what you want to create in your culture is an earning mindset. As in athletics, an earning or performance mentality exists in an organization when there is a certain amount of pressure, tension, or positive anxiety.

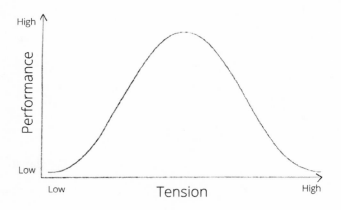

Positive Tension

As demonstrated in the graph, in an organization where no pressure or tension exists and where not much is asked of employees, there are lower levels of performance. At the opposite end of the spectrum, when there is so much pressure in an organization that employees are afraid (typically top-down organizations—think 1950s-style management), employees are not nearly as concerned with being productive as they are with self-preservation. They are more concerned with not getting fired or yelled at. Additionally, in a culture of fear, employees are so consumed with not failing that they tend to play it safe. This stifles the potential for innovative ideas, risk taking, and process improvements. A culture of fear also leads to a lot of politics and zero sum thinking, i.e., if you die, I live. In leadership, there is an art to creating an organization where you can have high expectations of performance throughout the organization without creating a culture of fear.

No one wants to fail, of course. But the truth is that the potential for failure causes people to try harder to succeed. By creating the potential for failure, we trick ourselves into trying harder. In my experience, when people have to work hard for something, there is a greater sense of accomplishment, satisfaction, and pride when they succeed.

How people respond to failure is critical. Research[3] shows that the mindset of a person experiencing failure is the most important indicator of how they will

---

[3]   https://hbr.org/2013/03/how-you-can-benefit-from-all-y

respond to anxiety, tension, or pressure. People who fail repeatedly tend to develop persistence in the face of challenges. They develop a habit around failure that provides them with a mindset of toughness and a resiliency toward anxiety.

> **It is your responsibility to teach your team to operate with this powerful earning mindset.**

Mindset becomes an important factor in the success of employees. In his book *Why Employees Are Always a Bad Idea*, Chuck Blakeman differentiates between employees and stakeholders. Business coach Steve Chandler talks about the owner vs. victim mindset in his book *Reinventing Yourself* (below). In her book *Mindset*, Carol Dweck talks about the difference between a fixed mindset and a growth mindset. What all these theories have in common is the concept that a person's mindset is a choice and can therefore be taught.

Stakeholder/Owner Mentality	Victim Mentality
Independence	Dependence
I can	I should
Future-based focus	Past-based focus
Responsible	Blame and finger pointing
Delegate	Micro-management
Direction and focus	Rudderless wandering

Owner vs. Victim Mentality

In my experience, this ownership mindset can and should be taught and reinforced because most employees haven't grown up with repeated exposure to basic business concepts. As a leader in your organization, it is your responsibility to teach your team to operate with this powerful earning mindset.

Developing an earning or ownership mentality throughout your workforce does a number of positive things for your company. First, when your leadership team is transparent, you send a message of respect and you build trust, which, as I mentioned, is the core of culture. Business education causes your employees to look at the company like an owner does. They become more conscious of waste and get in the habit of seeking and sharing ways to reduce inefficiencies. When all members of a company have the eyes and ears of an owner, they begin to treat each other as partners, with a spirit of maturity and mutuality. Lastly, there is much more credibility in this new open and honest culture.

So how do you do it? How do you teach employees about business and finance, especially if you're hesitant to share detailed financials with them? My business partner, Tom, and I have written a new book, *Profit Works*, which goes into more detail on how to share financials, but I've included a few key points here to help you as well.

There's nothing magical about it, but it's important to remember that less is more. Whoever is doing the teaching needs to be dynamic, and they need to have credibility. Surprisingly enough, this is not an exercise that should be delegated to your financial person. I actually discourage this, as they often venture into complex terminology and concepts without realizing it, and then they've lost the crowd.

Instead of looking at business literacy training as just sharing financials, it is important that your employees understand what your intention is, why you are going down this path, and ultimately how you as a team and they as individuals will benefit from knowing and using this information. Show them the potential for where this training will take the company. They need to see the big picture of not only your intentions, but also what's in it for them and for the entire team if they follow you down this path.

Many companies make the comparison of business to a game, where profit is the score at the end of the game. The game analogy (keeping score, etc.) makes the process less threatening than just sharing stark financial statements and often helps employees embrace the idea more easily.

When we teach business literacy, we use very simplified versions of financial statements to clearly illustrate the three elements of an income statement (sales minus expenses equals profit), the three elements of a cash flow statement (cash-in minus cash-out equals change in cash), and the three elements of a balance sheet (what you own equals what you owe plus what you really own). As your team becomes more familiar with these statements, you can introduce more advanced concepts. Ultimately though, we want to remember the KISS rule: keep it super simple.

	20XX	%
SALES		
– EXPENSES		
= PROFIT		

Simplified Income Statement

Your goal is to create a strong link between your employees' activities and your lagging financial statements. Keep the training simple by focusing on the measurables that your employees really care about and can affect.

Remember, your goal is not just to share the financials in a one-way lecture or an unappealing presentation of "how we did last quarter"; these teaching moments are great opportunities for employees to begin truly owning the numbers, which is why we include a "who" column on every scorecard. The person with the greatest influence over each measurable should own that number and report on it. This ownership is a key tool for applying some pressure or tension in your culture, as it causes your employees to think about and discuss their opinions. Ownership creates positive tension that helps employees learn and grow.

> **Develop the habit of communicating results with your workforce on a regular, formal basis.**

Leaders in the best companies continually teach employees about business and finance. This is why we suggest you develop the habit of communicating results with your workforce on a regular, formal basis. Many of our clients map out a formal internal communication game plan each year with specific live events, food, recognition, celebration, and other engagement tools that help them reach out to their employees on a regular basis. This is a critical piece of the puzzle for successful employee engagement.

Teaching these concepts and sharing financial information will not be successful if you do it just once. In fact, if you start down the business literacy path and then quit, you will actually do more damage to your credibility than if you hadn't done anything. You will be perceived as having just undertaken another flavor-of-the-month initiative.

As your team gets more comfortable with driving the measurables on a regular basis, you will undoubtedly encounter a measurable from time to time that is consistently out of whack. A great tool to get everyone focused on improving that number is to set up fun Challenge Rocks. These games are often called by other names, are usually 90 days long, and can be company-wide or departmental. When you design a Challenge Rock, it's important to not overthink it. Simply set up a challenge to move the measurable from X to Y in 90 days. The path to what winning looks like must be very clear. And when the team wins a game, celebrate! See the nearby graphic for an example template you can use to help design your Challenge Rocks.

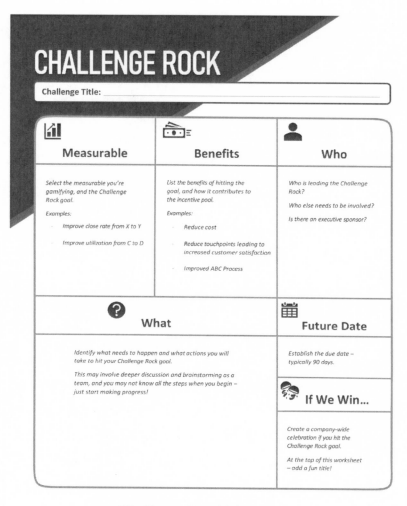

Challenge Rock Template

Games are a great tool because they blend a financial focus with a culture of participation. It's that healthy and smart thing again. Soft and hard. Yin and yang. Balance. They're fun, and they're also designed to drive improvements in the business that will help employees actively participate and win in two ways. First, they win through the celebration at the end of the game. Second, they help engage the team in funding an incentive plan, which I'll talk about briefly below.

I must caution you with the games: even though they are fun and add an element of camaraderie and accomplishment to the culture, don't feel the need to wrap a game around every measurable you have. If fun is not part of your culture, don't force it. There's nothing more awkward than telling your employees that they have to have fun. It must happen more naturally than that. If games and challenges aren't your thing, consider prioritizing the improvement goal as someone's quarterly "Rock."

As you begin to engage your employees by teaching business literacy and providing Tension Tools™ like measurables, scorecards, Level 10 Meetings, and Challenge Rocks, it is also effective to design and implement a simple incentive plan and to present it as a win-win situation. We all win when the company wins. Although we find that most employees are not motivated by money alone, an incentive plan sends a message of shared goals, earned rewards, and enhanced team performance. In *Why Employees Are Always a Bad Idea*, Chuck Blakeman says that because stakeholders participate in profit creation through changed behavior and profit improvement efforts, they should also participate in an incentive plan. Although not having an incentive plan is not a deal breaker, designing a simple and effective incentive plan helps you establish credibility for your initiative and draws the attention of any fence-sitters in your organization. If we can get the 50 percent of your "disengaged" employees to engage because there is an incentive plan, then I'd score that as a win.

> **Many incentive plans become entitlements because there is such a weak link between the activities of the employees and the financial results in your company.**

It's important to note that many incentive plans become entitlements because there is such a weak link between the activities of the employees and the financial results in your company. In order for this not to occur, your incentive plan needs to be simple and discussed frequently, at least quarterly, within your internal communications game plan. It can't just be a once-a-year message. Done right, a simple cash-based incentive plan is a great opportunity for leaders to reconnect the dots for everyone. A great incentive plan also reinforces that everyone in the company should always be looking to reduce inefficiencies and recognize and seize new opportunities for growth. We discuss how to design simple, self-funded incentive plans in detail in our book *Profit Works*.

COMPANY PROFIT (Trigger = $1,000,000)	INCENTIVE POOL (30%)	COMPANY PROFIT (after payout)
$1,000,000	$0	$1,000,000
$1,500,000	$150,000	$1,350,000

Sample Incentive Plan Design

Focusing too much on the financial payout of an incentive plan also diminishes its attraction for employees. It may be perceived as a hollow carrot. We use the terms *smart* and *healthy* to help combat this. As we've discussed, smart and healthy are the yin and yang of business; you've got to have both. The *smart* side of the incentive plan is the financial payout. Employees certainly love the payout. In over twenty years helping companies design incentive plans, I've only seen one occasion where an employee didn't want the payout, and that person soon after decided that they weren't a fit in the organization. But I've found there is a fine line between celebrating by providing a financial reward for the team and making it the only reason you are engaging with the employees. The *healthy* side of the incentive plan is the intrinsic value your team feels when you win. It's that sense of camaraderie, teamwork, accomplishment, and fun that comes with setting a goal and accomplishing it as a focused team. As a leader, it is important that your motives are pure when it comes to the incentive, and this purity needs to be expressed frequently so your employees know your aim is true. It all goes back to trust and credibility.

In addition to financial rewards, many companies include non-financial rewards to recognize employees, have some fun, and create some healthy internal competition. There are multiple books on this topic and one we like is Bob Nelson's *1001 Ways to Reward Employees*. Rest assured, done with an honest heart, an effective, straightforward, and transparent incentive plan will absolutely engage your workforce.

Chapter 5

Your Vision Works

Implementing an operating system like EOS as well as the employee engagement tools found in The ProfitLink Solution™ are proven methodologies that not only improve the financial performance of your company but also create a winning culture of trust. Leaders who commit to the principles outlined in this short book can transform their companies in a very short time. When there is clarity among your leadership team, and that clarity is communicated regularly to your workforce, it leads to credibility and trust within your culture. When you have a culture built on that firm foundation of trust, you'll see a clear path toward the engagement of everyone in the organization. It's truly incredible what your team can do when everyone knows where to look and is rowing in the same direction.

> **Using intentional tools that create healthy tension in your organization, your numbers will move in the right direction. I guarantee it.**

When the leadership team speaks the same language, walks the talk, and holds each other accountable on a regular, formal basis, using intentional tools that create healthy tension in your organization, your numbers will move in the right direction. I guarantee it.

Since we first published this book in 2015, our business model has continued to evolve. Today we implement The ProfitLink Solution™, illustrated below, which follows three steps:

1. Implement an operating system.

2. Design The No-Entitlement Incentive Plan™.

3. Implement Tension Tools™.

This process is detailed in our new book *ProfitWorks: Unravel the Complexity of Incentive Plans to Increase Employee Productivity, Cultivate an Engaged Culture, and Maximize Your Company's Potential.* A free chapter of *Profit Works* is included in Appendix B.

ProfitWorks

OPERATING SYSTEM
- Clear Vision
- Execution & Accountability
- Healthy Culture

THE NO-ENTITLEMENT INCENTIVE PLAN™
- Establish Trigger
- Determine Share
- Decide Who

THE PROFITLINK SOLUTION™

TENSION TOOLS™
- Profit Education
- Scorecards & Measurables
- Challenge Rocks

www.**profitworksllc**.com

Unravel the complexity of incentive plans to increase employee productivity, cultivate an engaged workforce, and maximize your company's potential.

AFTERWORD

You may be wondering how our Peruvian Clarity Trip that I shared at the beginning of this book ended. We arrived safely at our next campsite and were able to rehydrate and relax before dinner. I will say that Tom certainly lost his sense of humor and Oliver kept his distance from us for a few hours to let us recover, giving us some space before he began to make "deposits" back into our trust account. A beautiful thunderstorm kept us in our tents all night, and we awoke with a fresh perspective and renewed energy. We finished the hike a few days later, climbing around Machu Picchu, having what can only be described as a spiritual experience. We flew home on the same page yet again, and with many new ideas to pursue toward achieving our vision of what ProfitWorks could become.

I also mentioned at the beginning of this book that Tom and I successfully conquered Mount

Kilimanjaro on September 29, 2014. The "high" that we experienced was truly even higher than the summit itself.

Our trek was a predetermined reward for accomplishing our business goals. We had formalized our business arrangement less than one year earlier. We are well-versed in the best practices of EOS as well as employee engagement training and tools. By "practicing what we preach," so to speak, we exceeded our goals. We took this trip not only in celebration, but also as our retreat and Clarity Break™. Soon after the trip, we planned the short-, mid-, and long-term strategies that would support our future financial success and fulfill our personal mission to help other entrepreneurs.

Even on the mountain, the principles of EOS came into play. Halfway up our climb, our guide left us. To be fair, his wife was having an emergency appendectomy. But it did cause us more than a little concern; we still had 6,000 vertical feet to go (the peak is at 19,341 feet). The assistant guide spoke very poor English; no one else spoke any. How would we communicate in an emergency? How would we get to the top? Who would manage the porters?

We shouldn't have worried. These guides understand that "stuff happens" and that their clients' safety is paramount to their livelihoods. Each adjusted to their newly assumed role in the Accountability Chart with ease. An Accountability Chart and Succession Planning in Tanzania? It was clear they had planned for and discussed situations like this. The Assistant Guide became the Lead Guide; the Head Porter became the Assistant Guide. Everyone just carried a little more weight—literally. Even with the language barrier, we clearly understood the new hierarchy and were immeasurably impressed by the transition. It made us ask ourselves, "How many businesses are braced for an unexpected change in leadership, or for a change in the business landscape due to external forces beyond their control?"

We returned renewed and with clarity of vision and a commitment to new goals. We've set new travel adventures in our sights, and these motivate us every day to stay focused and better support our clients.

My passion is to help entrepreneurs get everything they want out of their businesses. Sharing these experiences with you, as well as a proven process that will help you create a vision and achieve it—for yourself and for everyone in your company—is what *Vision Works* is all about. I'm happy to say I've seen it work for hundreds of my clients as well as for my own company. Vision works when we implement the proven tools to awaken an earning mindset, bridge that missing profit link, and cultivate the untapped potential that exists within our organizations.

I wish you success on your journey, and I encourage you to find and interact with ProfitWorks via our social media platforms. I look forward to continuing the dialogue.

ACKNOWLEDGMENTS

Thanks to the late Donald A. Freytag, my father, for introducing me to the importance of business acumen at all levels of an organization. Thanks to Mom for encouraging me, teaching me discipline, and always emphasizing the positive. Thanks to Christine, Alec, Sophia, and Ethan for your support of my passion. Thanks also to the EOS Implementer community, my brothers, and my team for your encouragement and support.

APPENDIX A

Mindset Scorecard

Mindsets	1	2	3	4	5	6
1 Transparency	You believe that only the owners should know about the financials of the company. They're too overwhelming as it is.			You're open to sharing financial information with people, but are worried they won't understand it or that they might share it elsewhere.		
2 Teamwork	You don't have time to worry about everyone else. It's every man for himself. People will earn based on their individual effort.			You recognize great teamwork is possible, but only with lots of work. You're not sure you have the right leaders to inspire strong teamwork.		
3 Growth	You worked hard to get where you are and you aren't ready to share profits with people who don't own the business or put in as much work.			You want to grow and have tried a lot of things, but nothing seems to be working. Growth just doesn't happen here. You can't figure it out.		
4 People Matter	You know people are important: they drive profits and provide a return on investment for the company, but investing in them seems fruitless.			You know people are your best asset. You know they have the capacity to understand how profit works, but you need tools to help them.		
5 Operating System Discipline	You know everyone wears lots of hats and pitches in to do what needs to be done. You all work really hard and use a lot of common sense.			You've tried so many systems, but are frustrated with your people, your profits and a lack of control over your business. Nothing sticks.		
6 Data Discipline	Your financials and data are pretty disorganized and outdated. Sometimes you spend money in a reactionary way or on frivolous things.			You have decent, somewhat organized financials; you study the data and publish a budget every year, but you rarely stick to it.		
7 Earning	You don't think incentive plans change behavior permanently, but people feel they deserve them. A fair salary should be motivation enough.			You know incentive plans can change employee behavior, but the design & administration are complex and time consuming. They just fizzle out.		
8 Ownership	If people work hard, they deserve a bonus & you'll give them one. You pay fairly, give regular raises, often tied to tenure.			You pay fairly & try performance-based incentives. When people don't hit goals, you may pay out anyway, even when you haven't made money.		
Scorecard	➡	➡	➡	➡	➡	➡

Mindset Scorecard

Name:	Date:	A	B

7	8	9	10	11	12		
You don't think employees need to see the financials; they just need a target to hit. People only care about money & they need to do their jobs.			You know that when people have good information, they make better, more informed decisions. It's important that the company is transparent.				
You have effective teams and teamwork is fine. Team health stuff is silly; it would be easier if people just showed up and did their work.			You know effective teamwork is key to successful business. When teams achieve, there's a culture of pride, celebration, confidence and growth.				
Your business is stable: generating predictable cash flow allowing owner distributions/reinvestment. You don't want to disrupt your cash cow with changes.			You have a Growth Mindset; when the company wins, you all win. As you include people, they see growth. If you're not growing, you're dying.				
You pay people for their time and contribution: a transaction that works for all. If someone's not happy about it, they can work elsewhere.			You care deeply about people & teach them how to get everything they want out of life. You touch the lives of many people through your work.				
You track data: measure your people. They know what to do & there are performance measuring systems in place. You're organized & efficient.			A company can't improve or see growth using multiple operating systems, so you run one OS; it's the foundation for a great incentive plan.				
You have timely and accurate financial information and measure anything that can be measured. Your financials are detailed and complex.			You have timely, accurate data; track leading & lagging measurables at all levels. Scorecards are visible & teams use data to make decisions.				
You have incentive plans in place and employees know how to earn bonuses. You follow industry best practices & talk about it at year's end.			You experiment with ways to motivate. You seek best practices & look for new solutions. When you win as a team, you reward & celebrate together.				
It's at the discretion of the management team to decide who gets what at the end of each year. You're not giving up that control.			You believe in a simple, transparent, motivating incentive plan where everyone has control over their own earning ability.				

➡ ➡ ➡ ➡ ➡ ➡ ➡ ➡

APPENDIX B

Sample Chapter from Profit Works

PROFIT WORKS

Unravel the Complexity of **Incentive Plans** to
Increase Employee Productivity,
Cultivate an Engaged Workforce, and
Maximize Your Company's Potential

Contents

INTRODUCTION

This book is for entrepreneurs and business owners who want to learn how to appropriately incentivize and reward employees for their efforts to make your organization more successful. We use the term "appropriately" because many incentive plans just don't work; they pay out too much (wasted money) or too little (not motivating), they aren't fair, they become expected (i.e., an entitlement), and most of the time, they are too complicated. Regardless of your company's size, this book will give you simple tools and philosophies to design and maximize your incentive plan.

Like so many of you, we recognize that we are standing on the shoulders of giants with this topic. We appreciate those mentors, influencers, and visionaries who shared their time and expertise with us along our journey. We have provided further reading and resources in the back of the book and we strongly encourage you to tap into these.

This book combines and simplifies the research and our experience. We hope it will inspire you to consider different alternatives and will provide you with specific ideas to create the best incentive plan for *your* organization.

In this book, we use the terms "we" and "you" intentionally: "we" to represent our knowledge and experiences; "you" meaning, well, you. We want you to know we are truly a part of your team as you go down this path. We are passionate about helping entrepreneurs. This is a tricky topic, and at the end of the day, we recognize there's no silver bullet for incentive plans. Know that we are here to help you along the journey.

In this book, we also will use the term "incentive" generically to mean any extra money that is earned by an employee as a result of their changed behavior. This could be profit sharing, an incentive for hitting a certain target, gainsharing, or sales commissions.

Ultimately, recognize that whatever incentive plan you choose to implement, it is one more tool in your toolbox—a powerful tool, but still just one tool. Implemented effectively, the incentive plan is another lever that will help your company increase employee productivity, cultivate an engaged workforce, and maximize your company's potential.

Chapter 1

Why Profit Works

Since 1996, when we first founded ProfitWorks, we have asked employees, "What percent of sales do you think profit is?" Their answers may surprise you; most employees think bottom line profit is 30–50 percent of sales! While those results would certainly be wonderful, they are not common for most businesses. Upon seeing their employees' answers, one business owner exclaimed, "Are they out of their minds? Do they think I have a money tree in the backyard that I just shake when I want to make more money?"

If your experience is like ours, you know that profit percentages are usually in the single digits, and that profit is incredibly precious. Unfortunately, most employees don't think about this fact as much as you do. They certainly don't see profit numbers as often as you do, if at all. They don't feel connected to profits, and they commonly believe profit is something only the owner or executives need to worry about. Profit is powerful, though, because it funds growth, provides investors and owners with a return, and creates opportunities for employees.

You may have heard profit referred to as the "score at the end of the game." The comparison of business to a game makes it fun and accessible for everyone involved in a company. The game metaphor makes profit the first place trophy that stretches you and your team. The potential for profit can encourage a competitive spirit and the potential for everyone in a company to win (does anyone like to lose?). The fact that profit is typically small, hard to generate, and easy to lose creates what we call positive tension.

Positive tension is that level of anxiety where people are most productive and motivated. The objectives are not so overwhelmingly difficult or unachievable that no one tries. Conversely, they are not so easy that no one cares or puts in any effort. Think

Positive tension is that level of anxiety where people are most productive and motivated.

about if you tried out for an NFL team: making the team is probably not going to happen and as a result, you're not going to be motivated. (Well, you might be motivated to avoid getting hurt.)

Alternatively, think about your state's DMV: there is no motivation because there is no tension, pressure, or anxiety. Each of you will need to find that optimal level of positive tension in your company. Focusing everyone on profit is a great way to do that.

PROFIT WORKS FOR EVERYONE

Profit works for owners and investors. The potential for profit creates positive tension to generate a return on investment for investors relative to the risk they have taken. If there is no profit potential, investors typically won't take the risk to invest in the opportunity.

Profit works for your external relationships. It creates tension for you as it pulls against what it costs you to provide your products and services. It stretches you to make smart decisions related to your sourcing relationships as well as to the investments you make to grow your company through innovation, geographic expansion, and new product or service development.

Profit works for your employees. When focused on profit, you have the opportunity to create that right level of tension and to increase opportunities for all of your employees (e.g., advancement, learning new skills, increased compensation). When focused on profit, your entire workforce can benefit by understanding this tension. It can create an incredible culture of winning, where everyone is focused on generating more profit.

In addition, we've found that companies win when their employees understand how they benefit from being part of a profitable company. They will see the source of new jobs, the opportunities for reinvestment in the business, and their own potential for growth. We've also found that employees are more motivated when they understand the consequences due to a *lack of* profit, from reductions in force (RIFs) to pay cuts to fewer opportunities for professional growth.

Successful companies understand the benefits of creating positive tension or pressure. Tension isn't a bad thing. According to the Yerkes-Dodson Law, performance increases with tension, but only up to a point. When the level of stress becomes too high, performance decreases. So, a moderate amount of tension creates the most buy-in and effort and therefore, the most productivity. Like a rubber band, you want to stretch your team to grow and to reach for something more than mediocrity. Believe it or not, most people want this.

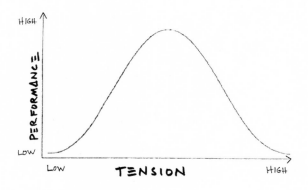

Instilling just enough tension in your culture encourages a higher level of performance. You and your team win when you implement simple and effective tools like weekly meetings full of intense debate and discussion on company issues, and when everyone is accountable. When there's just enough tension in your company, no anchors hold you back from higher performance.

Creating tension in your culture is a blend of art and science. The art is in what tools you decide to teach and how you choose to use those tools. The science comes from using a simple and transparent formula when you design your incentive plan.

Over and over again in client sessions, we hear executives discussing budgeting for bonuses, creating profit-sharing programs, and trying to figure out how to pay employees more so they don't leave for more pay elsewhere. In many cases, though, they're just winging it. There's no clear strategy or methodology for the design. It's often too complicated, not transparent, and has a high degree of subjectivity to it. You may be afraid to draw a line in the sand. You're often shooting from the hip. When incentives aren't truly "earned" and clearly understood, you create an entitlement mentality in your workforce. Entitlement is the death knell for a thriving culture and higher organizational performance.

One of our clients didn't want to follow a formula because she said it might "trap" her. She didn't want to reward underperforming employees. Our question was: "Why are they still with your company?" In the following chapters, we'll give you ideas on how to avoid feeling "trapped."

We encourage you to embrace the intentional philosophies and formulas we share with you in this book. We're capitalists with decades of experience working with hundreds of companies. We've seen what works and what doesn't work. Like you, we want your employees to add more value, to be happy, to be productive and to earn more, and not to get a bigger paycheck for no real reason.

Before we go further, let's provide an example of a simple incentive plan design that works:

- Imagine an annual profit trigger of $1,000,000. Above this amount, the employees can make more by participating in an incentive pool funded by their efforts. Below this, there's no incentive payout.

- Let's say 30 percent of every dollar above the $1,000,000 trigger goes into the incentive pool. If the company hits $1,500,000 in profits for the year, the incentive pool is $150,000 (30 percent x $500,000). It can be as simple as that. We'll talk about some ideas for how that gets distributed later.

COMPANY PROFIT (TRIGGER = $1,000,000)	INCENTIVE POOL (30%)	COMPANY PROFIT (AFTER PAYOUT)
$1,000,000	$0	$1,000,000
$1,500,000	$150,000	$1,350,000

Key Takeaways

- Most employees think bottom line profit is 30–50 percent of sales.

- Profit is the score at the end of the game and when everyone is focused on profit, you can create positive tension.

- Profit works for everyone involved in a company, including investors, external partners, and employees.

- Successful companies create just the right amount of positive tension in their cultures to create higher levels of performance.

- Successful companies commit to a simple formula when designing an incentive plan.

Thinking Questions

These are questions to help you slow down and reflect on what you read as well as to help you think about where your head is on the topics discussed in this chapter.

1. What do you think your employees would guess bottom line profit is as a percentage of sales in your company?

   _____

   _____

   _____

   _____

2. What are three examples of positive tension practices you've implemented in your personal life?

   _____

   _____

   _____

   _____

3. What changes in your own behavior and thinking have you seen as a result?

   _____

   _____

   _____

   _____

About the Author and ProfitWorks

Alex Freytag is the product of an entrepreneurial household. He has spent much of his business experience focused on his passion for being a hero to entrepreneurs. Between selling handmade James Dean T-shirts out of his locker in high school to becoming a Certified EOS Implementer, he ran or helped run five growth-oriented businesses before discovering EOS.

Drawn to EOS's simplicity and effectiveness, Alex has since devoted himself to helping others master this complete "way of operating" an entrepreneurial organization to help them get what they want from their businesses. An author and a sought-after speaker, Alex entertains, educates, and has introduced EOS to thousands of business leaders worldwide.

Alex resides in Columbus, Ohio with his wife, Christine, and their three children. He enjoys travelling, hiking, golf, scuba diving, and reading for pleasure.

If you're interested in implementing EOS and bringing The ProfitLink Solution™ into your company, please contact Alex at his company's website: www.alexfreytag.com.

ProfitWorks

Real. Simple. Results.

How do you harness your human capital,
set priorities, and solve issues?

Imagine Alex Freytag helping you set your vision,
gain traction, and create a healthy, functional team
by implementing EOS.

If you are frustrated by: a lack of control, poor revenue and
profit, your people, little accountability,
among other things...

...Tap into Alex's experience coaching

» **Over 200 companies**
» **More than 850 transformational sessions**
» **Over 8 years as an EOS Implementer**

Keynotes.
Workshops.
Presentations.

Tired of speakers who just give nice theories?
Need real, simple, practical tools?

Alex Freytag

uses his extensive practical knowledge and experience to engage your audience with the most relevant content and easy-to-use tools.

PROFIT WORKS

Unravel complexity.

Increase productivity.

Maximize your company's potential.

End entitlement.

Profit works for everyone: stakeholders, owners, and employees. It is the score at the end of the game. Discover how to design a self-funded incentive plan and maximize profit to help everyone win—especially you.

Does the money you spend through an incentive plan change employee behavior?

Do you have a bonus (entitlement) program?

Many organizations do not have enough positive tension. Some go too far; most, not far enough. Learn how to put a simple system in place to change behavior, activate an earning mindset, and maximize your company's potential.

Get your copy today at AlexFreytag.com

Made in United States
North Haven, CT
24 October 2021

10540144R10062